This Book Belongs To:

Gutsy Girl

gutsy \guht-see\ adjective: brave, courageous, daring.

Showing determination even when your heart beats fast, your hands grow sweaty, and you fear failure.

Dedications

To girls who, like Betsie, remind me to love hard and trust God: Laura, Leah, Lindy, Loraine, Lori, and because all of my friends don't have names that start with the letter L, Dusti, Kristi, Renee, Susan, Tomi, and Wendy. —A.L.S.

To my beautiful soul sister, Erin Margaret, I will always hold your hand, quench your thirst, and keep your secrets. And in loving memory of our brother Ben, see you in heaven! —B.A.W.

Gutsy Girls: *Strong Christian Women Who Impacted the World*
Book Two: *Sisters, Corrie & Betsie ten Boom*

ISBN-13: 978-1533021113

ISBN-10: 1533021112

Printed in the United States of America

Gutsy Girls

Strong Christian Women Who Impacted the World

Book Two:

Sisters, Corrie & Betsie ten Boom

Amy L. Sullivan

Illustrated by Beverly Ann Wines

Betsie ten Boom stared at her younger sister, Corrie.

"Corrie ten Boom, you cannot wear torn stockings on your first day of school! Your hat is missing. Your shoes are unfastened, and we are late for breakfast!"

Corrie listened to her sister's words and then slowly made her way down the stairs.

Corrie's siblings, Nollie, Willem, and Betsie, all went to school, but six-year-old Corrie ten Boom did not want to button up her shoes or wear new stockings or put on her hat. Corrie did NOT want to go to school.

Instead, Corrie wanted to stay home
in her funny shaped house with her mother,
father, and two aunts. Life at the Ten Booms' house,
19 Barteljorisstraat, was full of people and bursting with laughter.

"You must go
to school, Corrie!"
"Go ahead, take Papa's hand."

Papa walked Corrie to school, and she sat down
in seat 32, where she daydreamed about
what her life might look like
when she grew up.

But Corrie's life did not turn out as she imagined.

When Corrie grew up, she created watches in her family's watch shop, and Betsie managed meals and household duties. People trusted the Ten Booms to make excellent watches, but people would begin to trust them for much more.

During World War II, German soldiers invaded the Ten Booms' home country of the Netherlands and hung signs at libraries, parks, and shops, which stated:

NO JEWS ALLOWED.

"Get out of here. You don't belong!"

They forced Dutch citizens to give up forms of communication.

"Hand over that radio and telephone!"

German soldiers also controlled what was written in the newspaper.

"Of course that's true! It's in the newspaper, isn't it?"

It even became illegal for people in the Netherlands to sing their national anthem.

"Singing about your country is a crime."

But that wasn't all.

German soldiers planned evil things against people who were Jewish. In order to easily identify them and set those who were Jewish apart from other Dutch people, German soldiers forced Jewish people to wear the Star of David on their coats and ration cards around their necks.

Before long, German soldiers took many Jewish people away from their homes.

The Ten Booms could not believe this treatment of God's chosen people. Even though the Ten Booms' lives would be in danger for helping Jewish people, they decided to act.

In the top, top, tippy-top of the Ten Boom home, they constructed a secret place for people to hide.

Workers hid bricks and building materials in closed briefcases and old newspapers, and they sneaked them into the Ten Booms' house.

"No one can see the supplies we are carrying in."

"We must make this wall look real."

"If the Ten Booms get caught hiding people, they will be arrested!"

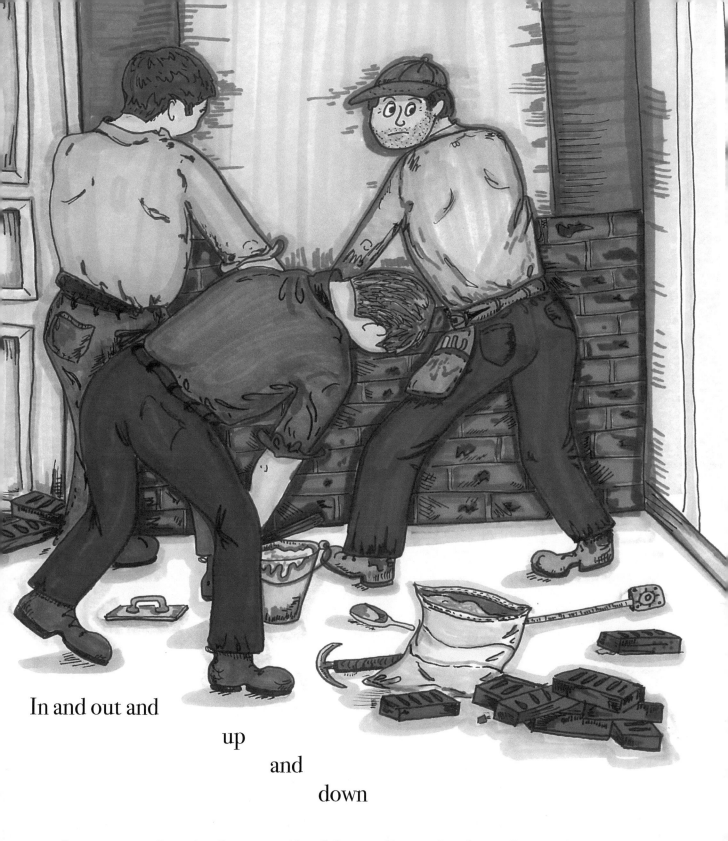

In and out and

        up

           and

              down

workers went for six days until a fake wall was built in Corrie's bedroom.

Behind the new bedroom wall, the Ten Boom family hid people: people who were afraid, people who were in need of safety, and people who were hunted by German soldiers. The hideout was small. Just how small?

It was only 23.3 inches deep and 7.9 feet long.
If you measure this book from edge to edge twice,
it's deeper than the Ten Booms' hiding place.
People scrunched down and crawled on their
hands and knees to enter the hiding place through
a secret sliding door.

The Ten Booms used a secret code when they talked to each other about the people they were hiding.

"The watches are safe."

This meant all of the people in hiding were safe.

They held practice drills and raced upstairs to the hiding place.

"It took you three minutes to hide. We must get faster!"

This meant practicing for raids in the middle of the night.

The Ten Booms prayed for people they hid and for the German soldiers, too.

"God, let them know You!"

This meant praying for people who were hurting others.

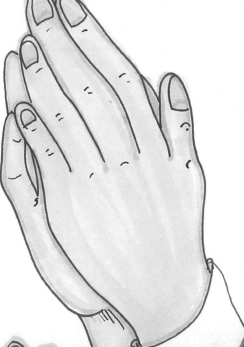

Only six people could squeeze into the hiding place at once, but over time, the Ten Boom family helped hundreds.

If every watch on these two pages was a person, they would represent the number of people the Ten Booms helped: 800!

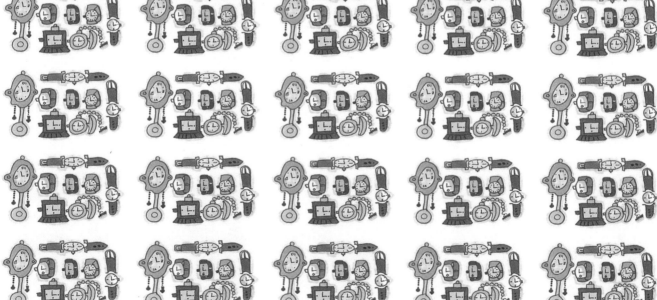

Then one day, a man told the police that the Ten Booms hid people in their home. German soldiers took the Ten Booms to a concentration camp.

This wasn't a camp with swimming, singing, and s'mores. A concentration camp was a prison. Prisoners were forced to work all day. They weren't given enough food or water or warm clothes. Families were separated from each other, and many innocent people died.

Already separated from their father, Betsie and Corrie prayed the two of them would be able to stay together. The sisters were not separated. They entered the same camp and stayed in the same barracks.

Bibles were not allowed in concentration camps, so Corrie secretly tied a tiny, worn Bible to a string and wore it under her clothes. She sneaked it past the guards, and then Betsie and Corrie shared God's Word with other women.

There wasn't much to be thankful for in the concentration camp, but Betsie reminded Corrie to thank God for everything.

"Thank you, God, that I am with my sister."
"Thank you, God, that many women can learn about You here."
"Thank you, God, for fleas."

Fleas? Fleas bite, and flea bites itch. All the women at the concentration camp hated the fleas that filled their straw beds, but fleas kept the guards away from Corrie and Betsie's building.

"I'm not going into barracks 28. That place is full of nasty bugs!"

Most days at the concentration camp were dark and sad, and in a group of thousands, Betsie and Corrie felt very alone. On days like this, Corrie struggled to pray, so Betsie prayed to God for both of them.

Then one day Betsie had several dreams about the future.

"Corrie, we will be released from this camp before the new year. I see a beautiful home in the Netherlands where Dutch people can live and heal from the war. After the war is over, there will be no use for concentration camps in Germany, but there will be a need for homes for Germans. I also see an old concentration camp made new. The buildings will be painted light green, and both flowers and vegetables will grow there. What was once evil will now be used for good!"

Corrie wanted to believe Betsie, but Corrie thought Betsie's dreams seemed too big to believe. One day, Betsie grew very sick and died. Corrie lost her dear sister whose faith was so much stronger, and for a while, she lost hope.

She thought Betsie's dreams were impossible.

Not long after Betsie died, Corrie was allowed to leave the concentration camp.

"Go home, prisoner 66730. You are free."

When Corrie returned home, instead of seeking revenge, she dedicated her life to traveling and teaching people about God.

Corrie met German soldiers and shared God's love.

"I forgive you!"

She traveled to 61 countries to talk about Jesus.

"Jesus can turn suffering into His glory!"

And Corrie even saw Betsie's dreams come true.

"Yes, this building needs light green paint AND flowers!"

As years passed, the world expected Corrie to show anger and seek
revenge on those who hurt her and thousands of others,
but Corrie refused.

Risking their lives to assist people who were Jewish
and underground workers, the Ten Boom family showed the world
that faith and forgiveness triumph over evil.
God gave Corrie and Betsie strength to forgive
and show others how to forgive.

That's gutsy.

Words for Gutsy Girls

1. **barracks -** a building or group of buildings used to house people or soldiers.

2. **illegal -** against the law.

3. **Netherlands -** a country in northwestern Europe where people speak Dutch; sometimes referred to (inaccurately) as Holland.

4. **raid -** a sudden attack in which something such as property or possessions are often seized.

5. **ration cards -** a card given by the government which allowed the holder to get food and other needed supplies.

6. **Star of David -** a symbol associated with Judaism.

7. **World War II -** a war which took place between 1939 and 1945. World War II is known as the deadliest war in history.

Sources

Corrie ten Boom: A Faith Undefeated. Directed by Robert Fernandez. Vision Video, 2009. DVD.

"Corrie ten Boom Biography," *Biography.com*. Accessed December 15, 2015, http://www.biography.com/people/corrie-ten-boom-21358155.

Nieuwstraten, Frits, Director of Corrie ten Boom House Foundation. Email to the author. April 16, 2016.

Smith, Emily, Corrie ten Boom Museum employee. Email to the author, 20 October 2013.

Ten Boom, Corrie and Elizabeth and John Sherrill, *The Hiding Place* (Grand Rapids, MI: 1971).

Historical Note on Corrie and Betsie

On August 19, 1885, in Amsterdam, Netherlands, Elisabeth (Betsie) ten Boom was born to parents Casper and Cornelia ten Boom. Soon after, siblings Willem and Nollie arrived, and on Good Friday, April 15, 1892, Cornelia Arnolda Johanna (Corrie) ten Boom joined the Ten Boom family.

Gutsy Girls highlights how the Ten Boom family hid people in their home, but hiding people wasn't the only way the Ten Booms served people during World War II. They also sought out other places for people to hide, administered ration cards, held prayer meetings, and provided money for those in trouble. No one is sure of the exact number of people the Ten Booms aided, but survivors estimate at least 800.

Both Betsie and Corrie remained unmarried throughout their lives. The sisters resided at the Beje (the nickname they gave their home) until they were removed from their house by German soldiers when they were in their fifties.

After Corrie and Betsie were arrested, they were taken to the Haarlem jail, Scheveningen prison, Vught Concentration Camp in Holland, and finally, the notorious Ravensbrück Concentration Camp near Berlin where over 96,000 women died.

Not until Corrie visited Ravensbrück in 1959 did she learn that her release from Ravensbrück was a clerical error. Only one week after Corrie was released from Ravensbrück, all of the women her age were killed in a gas chamber.

Corrie witnessed Betsie's visions come true, and for the rest of her life, Corrie continued to serve God by speaking and teaching about His love and forgiveness.

Gutsy Girls

Strong, Christian Women Who Impacted the World

Book One: Gladys Aylward

Book Two: Sisters, Corrie and Betsie ten Boom

Book Three: Fanny Crosby

Book Four: Dr. Jennifer Wiseman

Book Five: Sojourner Truth

For free educational materials for classrooms, churches, and families, vist the author's website, AmyLSullivan.com.

About the Author

Amy L. Sullivan doesn't always feel brave, but her picture book series, *Gutsy Girls: Strong Christian Women Who Impacted the World*, allows her to comb through history and steal wisdom from the great womenwho came before her. Amy lives with her handsome husband, two daughters, naughty dog, and lazy cat in the mountains of Western North Carolina. Connect with Amy at AmyLSullivan.com.

About the Illustrator

Beverly Ann Wines is an illustrator, painter, and art teacher. Beverly's art reflects who she is and what she loves. Beverly's art can be found in bookstores, homes, and galleries across the nation. You can learn more about Beverly's work by emailing her at Bvrlywines@aol.com or visiting her website beverlysartandsoul.weebly.com.

CPSIA information can be obtained
at www.ICGtesting.com
Printed in the USA
LVHW072254221118
597952LV00008B/156/P